HELP!

My Child is ADHD!

A Journey In Parenting an ADD - ADHD Child

By

Lydia L. Herrera

www.unleashyourchildssuccess.com

ISBN: 978-1-62517-087-3

For the gifts of patient support and unending encouragement,

I dedicate this book to my husband, Phil.

You continue to be my valued partner in life and love.

You make my day so happy!

Contents

Acknowledgments

I would like to express my sincere appreciation to Litzy Ledbetter, who kept reminding me to "Write the book!" Her belief in the importance of my story helped me see the book before it was written.

Sincere thanks to Belinda Mooney, whose inspiration and prayers over the years helped me stay the course.

AJ … you taught me how to be a mom. You are a hero in my life. I love you.

Christopher, without you, "our story" would not have been possible. I am so glad and proud to be your mom. I love you.

A Word From The Author

I want to take this opportunity to thank you for picking up this book. I think you will find it interesting. Since I know how busy parents can be, I did my best to make it short and to the point. Who has time to read a 200+ page book these days?

My goal in sharing my story is to give you hope as you raise your ADD – ADHD child. Also tucked into the story are ideas to help you in the day-to-day challenges you face. I've been there. I know what you are going through.

Above all, I want to remind you of this fact: you are a good parent. You have what it takes to help your child succeed. I truly believe if I can do it, you can do it!

I would like to know what you gained from reading this book. I hope you will contact me at lydia@lydiaherrera.com with your thoughts. I would love to hear from you.

Forward #1

With wit and gentleness, Lydia recounts her sensitive perceptions of the ups and downs, rewards and frustrations of life with her ADHD (Attention Deficit with Hyperactivity) child, Chris. The beginning quote sets the tone, "To have courage for whatever comes in life–everything lies in that." Those of us who have children with ADD/ADHD know that fortitude is one of many virtues that we cannot survive without. Since these wonderful, intelligent, and often gifted children are at the same time the most demanding people we will ever be in charge of, they pull out the best and sometimes the worst in us. Lydia refers to the daily "life in the trenches"–we can relate. It is a constant struggle to give them what they need, and at the same time help ourselves overcome all the flaws we see inside as a result of dealing with them. Sometimes it's just trying to keep ourselves from going crazy! There are other times when we have to exercise the utmost self-control not to say or do something to relieve the anger and frustration produced. Lydia shows how these times are balanced with others where they are so intellectually, emotionally or spiritually perceptive that we are left in stunned admiration.

Lydia has stated some really profound truths that I too have experienced and ring a chord in me. "As I look back, the very persistence that drove me crazy at times is drawing him toward his destiny." Likewise, her comments about acknowledging your strengths and letting go of weaknesses picked up from our parents are very helpful and encouraging. I have been blessed with seven children to raise. Two of my three grown sons were diagnosed with ADHD (my oldest) and ADD (my third son). My oldest daughter (our fourth child) was also diagnosed with ADHD. With all of these children in a family, the behavior and chaos is catching. I laugh and say that the rest who don't have ADD/ADHD act as if they do! Personally, I have had to work hard (and have too often failed) to maintain structure, to have firm and consistent consequences and to find their strengths and giftedness, keeping them active in those good things thereby naturally reducing the undesirable behavior. I found, like Lydia and others, that the more involved and immersed the children are in the intellectual, athletic and creative areas of giftedness, the less the deficit is a problem. My oldest son loves chess which he called "the ultimate game." He was able to study four hours a day when he was fourteen years old because he was so talented. My third son loves music and when he plays the piano, is completely focused. My daughter loves music, art and writing. Focusing on her gifted areas has helped her to excel.

From the scrapbook Lydia gave Chris to the Mother's Day Card he gave to her, the book is full of memories and practical solutions on how to handle challenges and the "downward spiral" that can happen when behavior and attitudes get out of hand. More structure, more consistency in everything, especially discipline and really pulling out their strengths and giftedness will call forth the best in our children. These will help in trying to live day to day a love that is based on not just feelings, but a decision. We have to love our child no matter what, through everything and we can! Reading this has brought up so many memories of my own children. It has renewed my hope that I can make a difference with all these children I've been given. I can see Lydia telling me, "persevere, hang on, and don't give up on them or yourself. With God's help you can and will do this work of raising and loving these incredible children and loving and supporting your grown children." Thanks Lydia–well done!

Belinda T. Mooney

Belinda T. Mooney is the author of the following books:

Leave Me Alone: Helping Your Troubled Teenager
Christ the King, Lord of History Workbook and Study Guide;
Christ and the Americas Workbook and Study Guide.

Forward #2

Lydia writes this book out of love, and the desire to offer hope to anyone raising a child with Attention Deficit / Hyperactive Disorder- ADHD. We are honored to write this forward for the book, for we not only know Lydia well, we are deeply linked to the Herrera family.

You see, we received our names as grandparents – Boomma and Boompa – because of Chris. He is our oldest grandchild. We are so proud of him. Through a set of events, our daughter became pregnant with Chris. She wrestled with keeping the child or not while she was pregnant. She finally made the decision to let her baby be adopted - but only if it were the Herrera's. Through prayer, much discussion and a bit of divine intervention, Chris became theirs. It was one of the most powerful days in all our lives.

So as Chris became a Herrera, we needed a different name than Grandpa or Grandma for us to define our relationship with Chris. One of our favorite movies, Mr. Hobbs Takes a Vacation, used the term "Boompa" to describe the Grandfather. We added Boomma, and the names have stuck. All our 14 grandkids call us these names today, and we love our names that are ours because of Chris.

Lydia does a wonderful job in her book of describing the frustrations, struggles and joys of raising a child with ADHD. This disorder (aptly named) occupies your life in a way that defies easy solutions or simple fixes. We adopted two children with ADHD ourselves, and know the challenges of parenting a child that cannot focus like most other children. As a result of our kids with ADHD, Linda went on to study Psychology, and became a Marriage and Family Therapist.

We found, as Lydia describes in her book, when raising a child with ADHD, on good days you learn to cope. On bad days you simply try to muster the courage to face another day. It is hard, but can be so rewarding. Parenting is about loving and giving love in ways you never imagined.

Lydia lays out the importance of persistence, learning, starting all over again, finding new ways, and the power of support and faith in parenting a child with ADHD. This all can lead to great rewards in our life… the rewards of watching your child become an adult, who knows that they are valued, loved and have an important place in this world of ours.

You will laugh, cry, and LEARN a great deal as you read this book. If you have a child with ADHD, you will also find one of the most important tools in parenting – HOPE.

Enjoy!

With Deep Affection and Love

Boomma (Linda) and Boompa (Jack) Conrad

Linda Conrad is a Marriage and Family Therapist

Jack Conrad is Manager of Faith and Health at Le Bonheur Children's Hospital. Jack is also the author of the following books:

Living Before Dying 2007
The Toy Box 2012

HELP!

My Child is ADHD!

A Journey In Parenting an ADD - ADHD Child

1

The Scrapbook

"To have courage for whatever comes in life – everything lies in that."

Theresa of Avila

As he got in his little black Honda, my heart was breaking. My "baby" was moving away. Tears rolled down my cheeks and the lump in my throat was so large, I could hardly breathe.

He was moving back to Southern California. The place of his birth. The place where he had grown up. The place where his good friends still live. The place that he considers home. We moved from California a year ago. Now at twenty-one, our son, Chris, was leaving our home. Probably forever. Although my heart was breaking, it was clear he was excited for the adventure. Who could blame him? We all have to take that leap at some point. This was Chris's time.

My husband, Phil, and I watched the car Chris had bought from his older brother turn the corner and slowly leave our street. I felt a heaviness in my chest. The sun seemed to dim a little. Phil and I turned and slowly walked back to the house arm in arm. As we entered the house, I looked around. Everything was the same, and yet it was different. I made my way through the house to Chris's room. Walking in, I couldn't help but chuckle through my tears.

True to form, his room was a mess. Chris had left so many things behind. On his bed were clothes that no longer fit and some that fit but didn't make the "clothes I'll wear again" list. There were some electronic parts that had been deemed outdated, a pen that didn't work, paper that had been tossed but hadn't quite reached the trash can. Empty hangers were everywhere. There were some toiletries on the dresser. "Did he forget those?" I wondered. His room looked familiar, but everything had changed. Chris was gone.

Tearfully, I made my way through his room to the bookshelf. There were several things there. I was curious. What "treasures" did he leave behind? As I got closer, I saw it. He had left behind the scrapbook I had so painstakingly created for his high school graduation. It chronicles his life from birth to graduation. I picked it up and cradled it in my arms. There are so many memories between those book covers. I sat on Chris's bed, afraid to open it. I just held it to my heart.

"How did we do it?" I asked myself. How did we make it to this point and still enjoy each other's company and love each other? You see, Chris is ADHD. This journey of parenting him has not been easy. In fact, raising Chris has been the hardest I have ever worked. I can remember many times when I wondered how I would make it through the day. Often, I would lie awake at night feeling guilty for an unkind comment or my bad attitude the day before. Life with an ADD or ADHD child is tough. I worry often about his future. Is he ready to be on his own? Will he finish college? Will he be employable? What will he do to support his future family? At times, the questions seem endless.

Again, I looked around the room and saw snatches of his life and snatches of my life spent for him. Many of the frustrations came flooding back. Many joyful memories came flooding back, too. It had not been twenty-one years of non-stop struggles. A smile came to my lips . . . yes, we had made it through and it was good. I was reminded of his Mother's Day card this year. Actually, it was a little book that had fill-in-the-blank sections.

> "To My Mother, I hope you know how much I love you and how grateful I am for everything you have done for me. But in case you need a little reminder, here's a book that explains just a few reasons why I am glad you are my mom.
>
> "I'm so glad I'm your child: For helping me feel special.
>
> "I want you to know I'll never stop being your kid, even when I'm away from you.
>
> "If you were a TV mom, you'd be most like: Gloria Delgado-Pritchett from *'ModernFamily'* – feisty and

> protective. And Marge Simpson from *'The Simpsons'* – always making us laugh.
>
> "As my mother, you've been my: cook, nurse, taskmaster, best friend.
>
> "If I had to describe you in three words, they'd be: loving, caring, funny.
>
> "Thanks, Mom, for filling our family life with joy, anti-boredom, and happiness."

Its message was so sweet and poignant. Knowing he would be moving soon, it was particularly meaningful. As I read his card that day, tears jumped out of my eyes and rolled down my cheeks. We hugged and cried together. Actually, we sobbed together. It was the most tender moment I have ever experienced with him.

I looked at the scrapbook again. I know what is in those pages. I pondered what to do. Several quiet moments passed before I settled into a comfortable position on Chris's bed and prepared myself to take a walk through his life again. I took a deep breath and began turning the pages.

My husband and I could not have imagined what life would hold for us. Of course not, the future is not ours to see. We can prepare ourselves as best as possible, even not knowing that the road will take many turns. Each turn is good if we see it as good and embrace it as good. One of those turns in the road is raising children. It is a challenge, especially with an ADD/HD child.

Our child is experiencing distractibility, inattention, disorganization and forgetfulness on a regular basis, at home and at school. The teacher has told us our child can't sit still, daydreams, or disrupts the class often and those behaviors are making it difficult for him/her to learn. We find ourselves feeling frustrated with our child when they bounce from activity to activity and can't seem to stay focused on anything for very long. Yes, these are some of the symptoms of Attention Deficit Disorder or Attention Deficit Hyperactive Disorder. I use the term ADD/HD to encompass both conditions.

According to the National Institute of Mental Health, ADD is a brain-based condition characterized by poor attention and distractibility. Add hyperactivity and impulsive behavior and you have ADHD. I call it ADD on steroids. More characteristic behaviors of both include: makes careless mistakes in schoolwork, does not seem to listen when spoken to directly, daydreams, struggles to follow through on instructions and finish chores, dislikes activities that require sustained mental effort, loses things, is frequently forgetful. ADD/HD can lead to poor school and work performance, lowered self-esteem and strained relationships. Studies show that ADD/HD affects three to five percent of preschool and school age children in the US. Boys are diagnosed two to three times as often as girls.

I suppose all of us exhibit some of those behaviors at one point or another. However, when our child exhibits those characteristics most of the time, we have a real challenge. Doing research to understand the condition helps a lot, and a formal evaluation with a qualified professional is important. However, the day-to-day living with our child is the real story. That's where the rubber meets the road. Christian author Chuck Swindoll wrote in one of his books, "The problem with life is it's so daily." As my husband and I raised our ADHD son, we have walked that "daily" journey. We have been in the trenches like you are now. Although it has been tough, it has also been a joy.

2

Who We Are Is Enough

"What you have to give is enough – if you give it with all your heart."

Chieko N. Okazaki

As we parent our child, we need to embrace who we are first and foremost. Our children are an extension of who we are. To embrace their magnificence, we need to embrace our own. Are we perfect? Oh, no, not by a long shot; but we can be the best version of who we are each day. That will be enough.

To do that, we need to take a long look in the mirror. What do we see? The blemishes? Oh, of course, we see those first, don't we? That little scar on our chin from a fall that happened when we were a child. We see the scars from the zits we picked at as a teenager. Yes, those scars are there and very visible; and makeup helps, but that only covers them. They are still there, and we know it.

How about the scars we don't see, but our self-image knows they are there. How about those? We know they are there because they bother us. They keep us in fear or off-balance. We try to hide them deep inside, but they can't stay down. They pop up every now and then. Actually, they rear their ugly head, don't they? When they do, we say or do something we wish we hadn't, not only with our family, but with others, too. We get in a situation that is awful –

sometimes downright ugly. "Oh, why did I say that?" we ask ourselves. If we are honest, we know it's the brokenness, the scars deep inside. Those scars can be our own feelings of unworthiness, jealousy, fear, laziness, or feelings of not being good enough, smart enough, etc. We know they are there; they are there lurking just beneath the surface. There may be situations in our past similar to what we just experienced and it brings up the same feelings, causing us to snap or respond in a way that is less than appropriate. You know those feelings. They are the ones that get us in trouble every time. They are the ones that have us asking, "Where did that come from?"

Since I am not a psychologist or family therapist by training, I am not qualified to give professional advice. However, I can tell you from experience that we need to find a way to go from where we are today and get to the point of letting go of those feelings – the brokenness that keep us from relating to our child in a way that is good, healthy, effective, and rewarding, especially when our ADD/HD child pushes the right buttons to make us crazy.

Raising our ADHD son has been the biggest challenge of my life. I'm sure you can say the same. Every day has been a roller coaster ride. That doesn't mean there haven't been daily moments of joy, but you know what I mean. I have had to grow as a person and a parent as we have raised Chris. His personality is opposite of mine and the ADHD has added an element of greater challenge. Although I appreciate so much of who he is, I have had to work with him in ways that have not always been comfortable for me.

I believe the most important thing for us to remember is that we are good, and we are worthy of the parenting role we have thrust ourselves into. Even with our weaknesses, we are good beyond measure. We were created for something special and that means we have been gifted in ways that can benefit ourselves and others, especially our children.

Now, that doesn't mean we are perfect, and that's okay. Perfect is not even a part of this conversation. Don't even think about going there. We are talking about the specialness that is you and me, the specialness that makes us unique. There are things about me and you that are so unique, no one else can measure up to that part of us. That means there is a responsibility to allow those special gifts to flow out of us and bless others. Those blessings are meant especially for our children. If we were created to have children, then our gifts were given to us for the benefit of those little people.

Let's start by identifying our uniqueness. Let's begin by recognizing the parts of us that are good, joyful, playful, inspiring. There are characteristics in us that others often comment about. Not the "You are so pretty" stuff. I'm talking about comments like "I like the way you listen"; "I enjoy your sense of humor, you are so funny!"; "You are thoughtful and kind. I like being your friend"; "You are a good mom, you are so patient." You know, *that* kind of stuff.

We can think about what we know is good about ourselves. I'm talking about the inner parts that resonate with others and our children. Are we caring and unselfish? Are we happy and satisfied for the most part? Do we have a sense of humor that people appreciate? Are we good and clear in communicating? Are we a good listener? What do we do well in relating to others? If we take some time to think about them, we can begin to appreciate our strengths and see them as gifts. Reflecting on them often can help us see ourselves as worthy and good.

These are our strengths. They are the part of us that brings joy to being a parent and will contribute to being effective with our children. Children are like sponges. They soak it up… the good, the bad, and the ugly. As we focus on our strengths and minimize our less desirable traits, we will go a long way in improving our parenting role and just plain loving our child. One of the keys here is not to be afraid to be the real us with our child. He or she will see the real us anyway. Sometimes, we are trying so hard to hide the ugliness that it just jumps out from behind our façade, whether we like it or not. We can get down on ourselves or we can chuckle and say, "There I go again."

Chris, our ADHD son, now that he is older, will look at me at times and say "*Really*, Mom?" It makes me stop and do a re-take. More often than not, he's pointing out the absurdity of what I just said. I look at him, he looks back with that incredulous look on his face and we laugh. It gives me a chance to rethink my comment, re-phrase, and then make my point clear. I know it is not a laughing matter when we yell something awful at our child. Believe me, I've "been there, done that." However, it's not the end of the world either. I have found that a heartfelt apology and loving hug can work wonders for a young child who did do something wrong, but got back way more than he deserved.

I call parenting "the agony and the ecstasy." Isn't that what it is? The agony of the challenges and the ecstasy in the joys. It seems one minute it is agony, the next minute, it's ecstasy. I remember thinking to myself several times over the years, "It's a good thing that boy is cute, or I would pinch his head off." He just did a 'no-no,' then instantly made me laugh or said something that melted my heart.

There were many times when I wish I had a really good parenting manual. Unfortunately, when you need the parenting manual, it's on the top shelf and you don't have time to read chapter seven anyway. Did I take parenting classes? Yes, and my husband and I learned a few things from them. A strategy here and there helps when you aren't confident and you second guess yourself. The problem is when the heat of the moment catches you off guard and you resort back to those automatic behaviors that just pop up. They're like a Jack in the Box. The little clown pops up and catches you by surprise. Those automatic behaviors can be kept down for a while, but they just pop up when you least expect them. Somehow, they make a mess of an already messy situation.

My husband calls those messy situations the downhill spiral. Mom yells, kid yells; mom yells louder, kid yells even louder. It's a no-win situation, and it goes downhill fast until someone puts a stop to the spiral. These usually ended badly. On some occasions, though, I found that the downhill spiral could end well. That happened when I stopped myself from responding in a negative way. Sometimes, I would walk away from the situation, taking our son's audience from him. When the situation was particularly odd and nothing worked, I would just say, "Do you need some loving?" At that point, Chris would stop, usually begin to cry, nod his head, and just melt into my arms. The heat of the moment dissipated and we could move on.

My husband and I owned a small business for many years. I helped with the accounting and general administrative duties, so I was also a working mom. Although I could work from home, it was not easy having to juggle the many duties I had to accomplish each day. More times than not, I was on the computer doing the accounting at midnight. It was the only time when I had quiet time and didn't have to check on Chris on a constant basis. I often did the laundry at the same time. So much to do, so little time.

There were so many times when I felt depleted. I discovered I had to fill my cup or I would get resentful and crabby. I had to find ways to refresh myself, and I had to give myself permission to do those things for me. I'm not really a "girly-girl," but I found an inexpensive nail spa down the road where I could get my nails done or have a pedicure. I treated myself to a massage when my shoulders and neck were bothering me. If the house was relatively quiet and every one was settling in for the night, I would steal away to my bed early and read a novel or magazine article I was interested in. At one point, I joined a bible study class at our church while my husband and our sons had a "boys' night" once a week. I enjoyed going out with a friend for coffee and dessert once in a while. Sometimes, just going for a walk or sitting on a bench at the local park to enjoy the fresh air was a welcome change of pace. I had to do something to "change it up" for myself or I would have gone crazy. My husband was very supportive in this area. He knew that a crazy mom does not make for a happy family. Thank goodness.

3

Our History

"God gave us memory that we might have roses in December."

Sir James M. Barrie

Our ADHD son is also adopted, so sprinkled in has been the adoption aspect. That hasn't been particularly difficult in our family. Probably because we have been so open about it. Chris has always known, and we've always given him lots of love. It has been a wonderful experience to love him as much as we love our natural son. Both are a lovely arrow in our quiver.

When Chris came into our family, he had several health issues right off the bat: allergic reactions to his formula, enlarged tonsils necessitating a tonsillectomy before age two, and a problem with toes pointing inward. All of these were identified and eventually resolved with a change in nutrition or medical interventions.

He was a "busy boy"; very active, always moving. He loved to play rough and tumble games with his older brother. The physical activity satisfied his need to move, move, and move some more. He would go from toy to toy, never fully engaging and he had a hard time sitting, even to eat. It was hard to keep him interested in puzzles, or coloring or any activity that required sitting.

Since he was constantly on the go, often he was on the go backwards. One Halloween evening, as we were trick or treating with neighbors, Chris was so excited. He was walking ahead of our group going fairly fast only backwards. Suddenly, he turned around and bumped right into a street-light pole. As first, I thought he had been knocked out. The hit was pretty hard. After a second or two on the sidewalk, Chris jumped up and kept on going. It didn't seem to faze him, he was too excited. He laughed with the other kids and was happy to be able to provide some comic relief to the hunt.

However, there were other times when walking backward was not funny, like when we would cross the street and he would be paying attention to me or a friend and not to the road ahead. Those were times when grabbing an arm and holding fast was all I could do to keep him safe.

In preschool, it became clear Chris was not learning as quickly as the other children in the class. However, he sure was good at recess! In kindergarten, his teacher requested we have him tested for learning disabilities. The results showed an auditory processing problem as well as ADHD. We looked for ways to help him. We did some play therapy. That did not make a difference for him. We also had him tested for speech delay. He participated in speech therapy sessions for a year. It helped a little, but I really think the auditory processing issue was causing his speech to be difficult to understand. I don't think he was comprehending what we were saying, so he didn't learn how to say some words accurately.

Even today, as an adult, I believe he doesn't hear some words clearly; not because he can't hear, but because the auditory processing problem doesn't let the sound get to the brain as it should. Sometimes I wonder how many adults have problems on the job or in relationships because of this type of issue. They are labeled dumb when, in fact, they are quite intelligent. They just don't hear and understand clearly so they appear not to be all there.

We were fortunate that the kindergarten teachers used a variety of activities that worked well with Chris's learning disability. They kept him busy with changes in activities throughout the morning so he didn't have to sit still for long periods of time.

In elementary school, Chris began to experience difficulties because of the classroom setting. Think about it: ADHD kid with an auditory processing problem has to sit in a classroom all day where the teacher talks – verbally instructs. Now, how in heaven's name was an ADHD kid like Chris supposed to succeed? "It ain't gonna happen," as my husband likes to say.

Those first years in a regular school were so difficult for him and for us. He had difficulty with reading and math, and anything that required reading, which is. . . everything. Chris would forget to ask permission to sharpen his pencil. He would poke the student in the next desk. He would daydream while the teacher was explaining a math problem. Every bulletin board distracted him from paying attention to a lesson. He couldn't sit still during quiet time. Life in a classroom with thirty other students was tough for him.

He is a fun and funny guy, so he rapidly became the class clown. If he were called on to read or answer a question he didn't know the answer to, he found a way to make the other students laugh. It made the teacher frown. It was not a good combination.

Third grade was the worst. By mid-year, his teacher was requesting we put Chris on medication to help him sit still and be quiet. She didn't care if he learned. She just wanted him to sit still and be quiet. To make life easier for her and, we hoped, for him, we did get Chris on Adderall. He took it until the end of the school year, and it did make life easier in the classroom. Sadly, though,

Chris was like a zombie. He was dull; his personality was suppressed. He ate very little, and he began to have nightmares. *Oh great,* we thought. He sits still and is quiet, but he's a zombie. How good could that be for him? We started to doubt the possibility that Chris could succeed at that school without being on medication. We had so carefully searched for a school we thought would be able to work with his challenges, but this one wasn't it.

4

Parenting Style

"There is no such thing as a perfect parent so just be a real one."

Sue Atkins

Much of our parenting style starts with the way we were parented and how that affected our character and our feelings about ourselves. What has happened to make us the parent we are today? How were we parented, and how does that affect our parenting style? Let's be real. We were programmed to a great extent to be the parent we are by the things that happened to us as a child. How our parents treated us, loved us, and disciplined us affect us today. Although we may have promised ourselves we would never do "that" to our child, have you noticed how automatically those comments or actions come forth in an instant? If you are anything like me, you stop yourself and say, *"How could I do that? I hated when my mom said that."* Or maybe it was a good thing your child did and your response was automatically loving and appropriate. You instantly recall a time when your parent responded to you in a loving way. You think to yourself, *"I remember when my dad used to say that to me. I loved it!"* Those are the moments when we realize how programmed we are. Yes, our little soul or subconscious mind took it all in and it was etched in our very beings like writing on wet cement. It appears to be there forever. Fortunately, we can grind off that impression from the concrete of our beings. It won't be easy, but when we parent our ADD/HD child, we cannot allow the automatic responses to control us. We have to be on guard and proactive so we don't make the current situation worse.

My own parents were quiet and low key. Although my parents loved me without question, they were not good communicators or demonstrative. We lived day-to-day as a family with little communication. My brothers and I were good kids, but I'm sure we got in trouble at times. I remember a lot of "just wait until Dad gets home." Obviously, Mom was not confident in her disciplining. When Dad got home, sometimes the infraction had been forgotten, or Dad got out the belt. I don't remember getting the belt myself, but I do remember my brothers getting a whack or two. Nonetheless, waiting for Dad to get home was hell in itself.

As I became a parent, my level of communication was better, but not much. I believe I am more demonstrative and warmer in my loving – more touchy-feely, so to speak; but real deep down communication has not been my strong point. Many of the disciplinary situations and difficult conversations with my children about important topics were either handled badly or put off.

In trying to work on my parenting style, I've had to look back on the things I remember growing up about the love, communication, and discipline. What was good? What was not so good? I have found myself resorting to the ways in which I was loved, talked to, and disciplined. At times I would do or say something that I wish I hadn't, then later thought that it reminded me of something Mom did or the way Dad would have handled the situation. It was almost second nature. It's amazing how imbedded these experiences are.

I came to the point of wanting to make a difference in my parenting style. One of the best things I did to help was to get in touch with the parenting style I experienced as a child. I really had to get real. No, I didn't have to tell my parents they made some mistakes. I know they did the best they knew how. But I did think about the things that were good and bad in my growing up years. I celebrated what was really good. And I have thanked my parents for what was good. I especially remember the Christmas when my father was dying of cancer. What could I give him as a gift? I decided to write a letter telling him how much I loved him and what I remember about growing up. He used to tell us a poem about doing our best. I included that poem in my letter. It was so good to share my appreciation with him, and let him know I remembered that poem. It was a great gift.

I also needed to acknowledge the not so good. Those cannot be ignored. When I acknowledged them and even talked about them out loud, they began to lose their grip on me. They lost the ability to control me ten, fifteen, even twenty years later. Oh, this didn't happen overnight, but it began to change as I thought about them, talked about them, prayed about them, and even cried about them. All of that was healing. It's a cleansing that took place in the inner me. As I allowed these experiences to be washed away, I opened up to new ways of doing things. The "automatic" wasn't so automatic anymore. I found myself thinking before acting. I got a chance to choose a better way. Sometimes, I chose to do nothing. It was still a choice.

In my husband's family, there was a bit of abuse. As a young boy, he saw physical abuse from his father aimed at his mother, and he heard a lot of verbal abuse. I recall many years ago when one of our sons was playing with a friend in our yard. My husband went to see what they were doing and found the boys playing with some broken glass. Although it was a potentially dangerous situation, my husband's reaction was totally over the top. Later, when we talked about the incident, my husband related that his reaction reminded him of how his father would react at times when he was a boy. It scared him. He could imagine himself becoming abusive, too. We talked at length about some of the abusive experiences he witnessed as a young boy and the anger that seemed to be just underneath the surface. Our conversations empowered him to determine in his mind that he would not follow in his father's footsteps. He relates now that whenever he felt himself becoming angry at one or both of our sons, he would remember those past experiences, get control of his anger, and think of a better way to respond to the situation.

Our ADHD son gave my husband many opportunities to choose a better parental response, as you can well imagine. There were many times when Chris's bike was left on the driveway, so Phil had to move it before he could park when he got home from work. Tools that Chris used never got put back in the toolbox. Chris would often forget to do what Phil asked him to do, and reminding Chris over and over again was so frustrating. It was hard to get Chris ready to go to soccer or basketball practice. There were so many instances that often drove Phil crazy, but he did his best to respond well.

I, too, have had my moments of less than perfect parenting. I mentioned before that I come from a family that wasn't big on communication. Many times, I was met with a "Because I say so," in response to my asking why I couldn't do what I wanted. I hated it. Any answer would have been better than that. It was like having a door slam in my face. You can imagine my dismay when I used that same response with our son a time or two. In talking with my husband about my disappointment in myself for responding in that way, I found myself commiserating with how my son must have felt, too. I could take myself back to my childhood, live the moment again, and resolve to change that in my own parenting style. And I did. However, it challenged me to open up and get better at explaining why a "no" was appropriate. I didn't always have a great answer, but it was better than "Because I say so."

I suspect most of us have had some of those moments when we did or said something and felt like our parent was inside us. When that happens, it's good to do our best to get in touch with the situation, talk it out with our spouse, a trusted friend, or even a professional. We will find ourselves being strengthened and empowered to change that dynamic. We will find the ability to stop ourselves in the middle of the situation, and think of a better response. We can play some scenarios in our mind with us reacting in a more positive and effective manner. When we have practiced in our mind, we will perform better when the real situation or one similar to it occurs.

I think it is necessary here to say, yes, we did discipline our sons differently. They are different personalities. What worked with one did not usually work with the other. Our older son was generally cooperative and easy to raise once he got past the terrible two's. A stern look usually worked to get his attention. Chris, of course, was more of a challenge. We did spank him on occasion. However, "time out" seemed to work best. It drove him crazy to be isolated. We made sure he was away from everyone and everything. We would set the timer and just ignore his cries or yelling until the bell rang. If it got really bad, the timer got re-set. It didn't take too long for him to figure out he needed to be quiet while in time out. It broke my heart, though, to sneak a peek and see him rolling on the floor or squirming like a bug. I'm sure it was hell for him; which, I guess, is the idea, right?

The best strategy in correcting him was to take him by the hand or arm, gently pull him away from whatever he was doing that was inappropriate and direct his attention elsewhere. Of course this required me to be diligent in observing him constantly. Frustrating as that was, it worked out better than allowing him the space to get in trouble. Talk about being an involved parent. Whew . . . that was constant.

Chris was always moving, and as a toddler, he preferred climbing to most activities. If I wasn't watching closely, I would suddenly be aware that he was very quiet. I would have to look for him. Usually, he was climbing a dresser or file cabinet trying to get to something we had placed up high and "out of reach." The key was watching him all the time. As an example, if I was diligent in observing him, I could almost see on his face what he was thinking as he moved toward a "forbidden" part of the yard or as he walked around the house with a crayon in his hand. Often, he moved with lightning speed, and I would have to run to catch up before he did something he, and I, would regret. I couldn't get him started on an activity and leave him for a few minutes like I could with his older brother. I found out quickly to do that would be courting disaster – usually small, but occasionally quite large. If I watched carefully, I could divert his attention from a situation that might turn into a problem. That was so frustrating for me; and tiring. I felt like I never had a moment's rest. I often fell into bed at night, totally exhausted, wondering what I was going to do tomorrow to make it better, only to have just as frustrating a day again.

Organizing my responsibilities helped a lot. I learned early on that anything requiring my full attention had to be done when Chris was either asleep, away with friends, or when Dad or older brother were around to help supervise him. He was just too busy to leave anything to chance.

Organizing toys, games, and other activities went a long way to help keep his frustration and mine to a minimum. Although he rarely was cooperative in putting things back in their place, "helping" him keep things in at least a general area was possible. It was so frustrating for him to want something that he couldn't find, so a general place was better than things all over the house. As he grew older, he got a little better at this. However, as a teen, his room often looked like a tornado had hit. I figured that pertained to most kids his age, so I didn't stress too much so long as the mess didn't cause major disruptions for the family.

Although it's hard to get ADD/HD kids to stop and think things through, setting up routine systems can help them become a bit habitual in some areas. My husband helped Chris with this when he started driving and would sometimes forget to take his wallet with him. Phil arranged a spot on the counter where Chris could leave his wallet and car keys. It required a lot of reminding, but eventually

Chris got the routine down. That saved him and us a lot of grief. When we moved to another home, Chris set up his own "spot" for his wallet and keys. It was a lesson well learned.

5

School

"The job of an educator is to teach students to see the vitality in themselves."

Joseph Campbell

When Chris was not succeeding in regular school, we began a frantic search for a good place for him, and stumbled upon homeschooling. That was a new concept for me; one that was certainly more challenging than any we had uncovered. I was very reluctant to consider homeschooling because I did not think I could teach my own child in all the basics. In an effort to be open to all options, I attended several homeschool conferences and learned a great deal. As we did more research, I came to believe that it was possible to teach Chris, and it seemed to be the best option for him.

So a new journey began. What I learned through homeschooling Chris has made a huge difference in his life, in our family, and in my life. The biggest lesson has been in learning how to work with Chris's learning style. This is a lesson I wish I could convey to all regular school teachers.

You see, at first, I wanted to teach Chris like I had been taught. Probably like every teacher in a regular school has been taught: teacher up front, good white board, markers, and lots of paper and pencil. Actually, I wanted to teach Chris in the learning style that is most comfortable for me . . . my learning style. Yup, that's what made sense to me . . . teacher using a white board, student taking copious notes and memorizing facts like crazy. Well, that's not what works for Chris.

My first challenge was to discover Chris's learning style and begin teaching to that style for his sake. As an ADHD kid, it's no surprise he is a tactile learner and needs hands on activities. Teaching him through talking was not effective. Reading was very difficult for him. He needed to "do" and "move".

My second challenge was to look for alternative teaching materials. I was amazed at the number of resources available for different learning styles. I had no idea there was so much out there. Walking into the bookstore at my first homeschool conference, I was met with row after row of booths with learning materials. As I walked around, it was clear the resources were there. Everything I needed to make this happen was right there.

There was a lot of encouragement from mothers who were currently homeschooling their children, many with special needs. Their enthusiasm and joy at teaching their children was a marvel. The closeness and mutual respect in the families was admirable. I wanted that. Mostly, I wanted Chris to succeed in school and this seemed to be the best way to make that happen.

The decision made, we embarked on a nine-year journey that has challenged me to the very core of my being, but would also prove to be in Chris's best interest.

We have used games, CDs, DVDs, books on tape, and computer activities to name a few of the strategies that worked for Chris. All of this is amazing stuff, and fun, too. We both had fun learning and just being together. I suppose a caveat of this is the time spent together. This helped me with my communication with Chris and others. When you spend 24/7 with someone, it's all about communication - communication about everything. He became my good friend in a lot of ways.

Was it all fun? No, of course not. There are some things that need to be taught that a game may not handle. It's hard to write an essay with game pieces. For the most part, though, the elementary and middle school years were all about games and other hands-on activities that helped him learn important concepts.

High school, you ask? Oh, yes, I homeschooled Chris through high school. It was especially challenging. There was a lot more reading and a lot more writing. Often, it felt like pulling teeth. He was not an ideal student, even with interesting resources and activities. However, together we waded through the difficulty of finding activities to fulfill the requirements for a high school curriculum that kept him engaged.

Whenever I was frustrated and questioning if this was a good thing, I had to remember that the classroom setting is not a match made in heaven for Chris. He has commented that the regular classroom had so many distractions, it was very hard to place his attention where he needed to. Because of this, he often worried about what others thought of him since he just wasn't getting what the teacher was saying. He tried not to let anyone know he was struggling. He calls the distractions of a regular classroom his "worst enemy."

Chris is quite stubborn; persistent, my husband says. That made most days harder. There were times when he just did not want to do a lesson. There were times when he would do just the very minimum. However, there were times when he was so engaged that he did not want to stop working on a lesson or project. I am reminded of the time he was studying for his driver's license. Now, that was major interest level, as you can well imagine. He read that handbook and studied the questions and answers like a trooper. He asked me to quiz him to see how well he was remembering all that he studied. He also had to attend an actual class. He sat in front to minimize distractions and did his best to stay focused on the teacher and the lesson. After a week of ardent study, he took the exam and missed only one question. He was so happy. So was I. That experience gave him confidence and the knowledge that he could succeed when he put his mind to it. As I look back, the very persistence that drove me crazy at times is drawing him toward his destiny. I am so glad we didn't medicate that out of him. Oh, did I mention we stopped giving Chris Adderall when we started homeschooling? We stopped the medication and got our little boy back; but I have to admit there were days when I could fully empathize with that third grade teacher who insisted he be on medication. It would have made my job much easier. The question is: How much would Chris have learned in a near-zombie state?

I understand homeschooling is not an option for most families for a number of reasons. However, I encourage parents to look for alternative ways to help their child succeed. It may be a different school environment, finding a good tutor, or it could be simply spending more time after school going over homework or engaging in additional activities to enhance their child's school experience.

One real concern I have for ADD/HD children is the fact that so many of them are in classrooms that do not accommodate their need to move and their educational needs. I think back to my own teacher days. I now believe every "trouble maker" was either ADD/HD, had a learning disability, or had a learning style different from the style most classroom activities are geared toward. I believe any child can be interested and engaged if the lesson is presented in a way that connects with their learning style. I also believe any teacher would be more successful if he or she committed to presenting each lesson in a variety of modalities. That would certainly require better planning and preparation, I know; however, what a blessing to have a classroom where each child, or most of the children, "get it." Can you imagine the brightness of the room with all those "light bulbs" going on in the students' heads?

How can parents be an advocate for their child in a regular classroom? First, they need to know the child's learning style. There are books on that topic, and there are services where an evaluation can be done. It is a worthwhile investment in the child's future. Next, parents can share that information with the child's teacher. If the child is assigned a special resource class or tutor, parents can ask about the activities that are used and how they fit the child's needs. Most special needs classes are planned for using different modalities. If the child is in a regular classroom and he or she just isn't getting the lesson, parents need to talk to the teacher to find out why. Is it laziness? Is it distractibility? Or are most lessons presented in a way that doesn't make sense to the child? I know this is asking a lot of a working mom, or one with several children; however, helping with homework using activities that do fit the child's understanding will make a difference. It's amazing how even one lesson explained in a way the child connects with will help him or her succeed.

I recall a time when I was trying to teach Chris a math lesson. It wasn't rocket science, but he just wasn't getting it and I was getting frustrated. I could tell he was trying, but we were going nowhere. He looked at me with those big brown eyes and said, "Mom, what if I do it this way?" He showed me on paper how he was seeing the math problem and how he was getting to the answer. It baffled me, but he got the right answer. To me, it seemed like he was going through the back door coming at the problem from the opposite direction. BUT, he got the right answer. It gave me hope. It opened my eyes to the fact that he could learn, just not necessarily in the way that made sense to me.

When Chris was learning the multiplication tables, I made index cards with answers to multiplication problems written on them. After spreading the cards all over the floor, I would say the problem and Chris would run to the card with the right answer. He could move and he had to think of the answer. This helped him remember while he was having fun.

Parents need to do their best to be an advocate for their child, making sure they don't do nothing and blame the school for the child's failure. Most teachers are willing to work with parents. They may not seek the parent out; a parent may need to reach out for help and not just at Open House or Parent Conference time. A call to set a time to talk over the phone or in person will get the ball rolling. An interested and engaged parent can only benefit the child so long as their attitude is positive and they show a willingness to be an active partner.

Every child's teacher knows when the child is struggling. The teacher will want to do what he or she can to help, but time is limited and others are clamoring for their attention. If a parent shows a willingness to be in a partnership, the teacher will go the extra mile for that child. However, parents need to do what they say they will do. Doing it with a happy heart is the only way to go. After all, it's our child who stands to win big time.

6

Lessons Learned

"We will be victorious if we have not forgotten how to learn."

Rosa Luxemburg

As my family and I have passed through the years with our ADHD son, I have learned some very important lessons. Of course, all of us in the family have had our level of challenge with Chris, so in effect we all have learned lessons. They are varied and I share those lessons in hopes that they may serve others as well.

Lesson #1 – Acceptance

"All I can do is play the game the way the cards fall."

James A. Michener

Unconditional love has been a key for us. It has given me and other members of our family the ability to see Chris's goodness and strengths even when we were frustrated and wanting to throw up our hands in despair.

I know what you are saying. "I love all my children unconditionally." Of course, you do. However, do you ever find yourself at times thinking you wish you didn't have to deal with all this ADD/HD stuff? I did. I felt terrible when I got those feelings. I felt guilty, like maybe I wanted my kid out of my life. Of course, the feelings would pass as soon as he did something really great or said something to make me laugh. The feelings would pass, as well, when I intentionally put a stop to them. However, there were many, many times when I wanted to run away and not have to deal with him anymore. Isn't that just awful? Yes, it is; but that is the real story. At times, I wanted him out of our life – out of my life - so my day could be easier for me. That was my selfishness and tiredness talking.

Oh, I love him with all my heart, but I wanted Chris to comply. I wanted a "Yes, Mommy" for every request so I wouldn't have to prod or cajole. Yup, I wanted the perfect kid. Well . . . near perfect. But my Chris wasn't perfect. And neither was I. As a mom, Chris brought out the worst in me. Rather, I let him bring out the worst in me. Or maybe, I brought out the worst in myself with my unrealistic expectations. You know, we can do that to ourselves. We expect things to be a certain way, and then we're really upset when that ideal situation doesn't materialize. At times like that, we are our own worst enemy. When we are accepting, we are less likely to sigh loudly or roll our eyes when our child isn't cooperating. We are less likely to flip out when things don't go our way.

As I write those words, I am reminded of my sister-in-law who is raising two autistic grandchildren. I am in awe of her positive attitude in spite of her situation. She is loving, patient and gracious, with those children. She laughs often. I believe she has learned to scale back on her expectations for certain behaviors from them. She delights in everything they do, and disciplines them with kindness.

My sister-in-law has the children involved in a lot of activities. They are often out in public bowling or at sporting events. Naturally, they don't comport themselves in ways "normal" children would, but that doesn't seem to bother her. She goes with the flow and enjoys their delight. Does her frustration show every now and then? Of course, she's human. However, her complete acceptance of them as they are is inspiring.

So, yes, I have had to learn to let go of my ego – my feelings about myself. Until I completely accepted Chris unconditionally, my ego was tied into the equation. I felt like his challenges reflected on me. If my child was not a good student and couldn't sit still in class or in church, I thought it meant I was a bad mom. If he couldn't read as well as the other students or stay focused in class, I felt others were judging me. "Oh, poor Lydia, her kid can't read." I imagined hearing "Poor Lydia . . ." so many times that I stopped taking him places. Now, let's be real. That was my self-image getting in the way. That was me judging myself and imagining others doing the same. I need not have bothered. Most people paid little or no attention or they just didn't care.

As you know, it is hard to have an ADD/HD kid in the family. Chris was different from the other kids. He often didn't fit in, except on the playground. He didn't read well, and his speech was difficult to understand at times. But the kids had fun with him outside of class. He runs really fast and he's very tall so he was interesting and he was funny and adventurous. I realized other kids accepted him and enjoyed him. It warmed my heart.

In letting go of my ego, I found I could accept that Chris usually had a different point of view; a different way of perceiving situations that wasn't necessarily wrong just different. Have you noticed that in your child? It's as if they see things from the other side of the mirror. I am amazed at the perceptiveness of Chris's comments and awareness. At times, he would mention a situation that occurred with some of his friends and comment on what he thought was going on. He would say something like, "I think she said that because her feelings were hurt." Or "I don't think he feels good about himself because he is so mean to others for no reason." I would be amazed that he had picked up on it. Sometimes he would make a comment about something I said or did that showed his ability to "read" my thoughts. It was uncanny. There's something really special about that. Often, his perceptiveness makes my nerve endings get all prickly.

As I have allowed my ego to melt away, albeit slowly, I have discovered that the way I see things can be changed or enhanced. I don't have to be right all the time. I may see things in a certain way and then Chris says something that opens my eyes. Suddenly, the blinders are pulled away and I'm aware of something that wasn't even on my radar. He has a way of gifting me with that different point of view. Chris is very observant, and I think his brain just works over time and in many directions until he boils down what he has been thinking into a succinct view that is actually accurate, but different. There is nothing wrong with that.

So, yes, there have been many instances when I have changed my mind because of what he has had to say. I have learned that I can just go with the flow. And his persistence is hard to push against. However, he is good about acknowledging when he is wrong if he can be convinced. Just like me. That means I have to think through my perspective, too, until I can convince him. A lot of this came about with his growing older. However, even at a young age, as I accepted that he had something worthwhile to share, and I gave him the gift of being open to his point of view, we could have an intelligent give and take.

Acceptance needs to be applied to ourselves as well. I believe it is easy for us as moms to try to be perfect, right? Yes, we want to be the mom who bakes the perfect brownies, has the cleanest, neatest home, looks great all the time, and our children are clean, bright and happy. Whew, that's a tall order. . . and it's unreal. We can have the best laid plans and they still fall apart. It's just part of having children, ADD/HD or not. Again, it's back to the ego. When we let go of our ego, we realize, thankfully, that we and our kids don't have to be perfect. It's the best gift we can give to ourselves.

Lesson #2 – Patience

"When you get to the end of your rope, tie a knot and hang on."

Franklin D. Roosevelt

Along with accepting Chris just the way his is, I learned to be patient. Did he always go to his room when asked at bedtime? No; most nights, no. But if I prepared him with a little verbal warning several minutes in advance, set a timer, and then 'helped' him get to his room and in bed, it worked much better. Did he eat his lunch or dinner in a time frame suitable to my liking? Not always, but I got to the point where I didn't mind him finishing his meal while the rest of the family cleaned up. Then he had to do his own dishes. He just dawdled often. Yes, even while eating. Eventually, he decided he would rather eat a little faster so he could have help with the dishes.

The dawdling could have been a real contentious situation for us. Actually, it was, until I eventually understood that it was more a matter of not being able to stay focused on the task at hand than his being disobedient. I had to come to the realization that I would have to check on his progress often. As he grew older, I was able to give him a list of what needed to be done and by when. He didn't always meet the deadline, but it made my job easier. However, I still had to check on the progress and quality of the work. When he was younger, more often than not, he would put it off until the last minute. If that happened, there would be a consequence: less time on his computer game or time out. Over time, he figured out that things worked out better for him if he got the task done right away. Hallelujah!

As it turns out, the list and deadline system has morphed into a strategy he uses now as an adult. If he has something that needs to get done, he makes sure it's on his list and he will work on it. It helps him not to forget, and has taught him to budget his time. As a college student, it is invaluable as he works to get assignments done in the midst of a busy school and work schedule.

As a young boy, Chris's mind would go faster than his mouth; the words coming out of his mouth didn't always make sense. So I learned to be patient when trying to get him to repeat or explain. He knew perfectly well what he was saying, but it often sounded like verbal shorthand. Incomplete sentences and jumbled words necessitated patience for both of us to make sure I understood. There's nothing worse than your kid trying to tell you there is a spider on the wall and you say, "Oh, good, honey." Ugh!

Many times Chris would just keep going and going like the Energizer Bunny. If he were into the activity, it was a real trial to get him to stop and move on to what needed to come next. Giving him a warning and a little transition time helped. He usually asked for "just one more" jump on the skateboard ramp, "just one more" time around the driveway on his bike, or "just one more" hand in the card game. So I started giving him a countdown. "Okay, Chris, you have five more jumps." Then he and I would countdown together. That really helped. I came to the conclusion that fighting wasn't going to get me what I wanted or needed him to do. In fact, more often than not, fighting to get it done only made things worse. I learned to do battle on the really important things, and relax a little on other small matters.

I believe I mentioned before that Chris was stubborn . . . IS stubborn. In some situations, it is not a good thing. As an adult, though, I know persistence will serve him well. I'm glad I didn't "fight" it out of him. Those were some the hardest times I remember with Chris. He would frustrate me no end. However, as I was patient, he would cooperate. As I spoke to him with a patient and kind voice, he reciprocated and cooperated. I found I would get farther with him when I remained calm and patient.

Chris often had a project he would work on. He would get an idea and try to figure it out. He didn't always think things through realistically, but he seemed to be very interested in how things work. We had to make sure whatever he wanted to take apart wasn't something indispensable because he usually couldn't put it back together again or he lost interest once he had taken it apart and knew how it worked. I recall a science project where he put together a radio. It was a simple kit, but had several electronic components. He worked diligently on it until he got to a point where he could see the end. Once he knew it would work and why, he lost interest. It was only a matter of a few more connections, but he could already "see" the finished product. It took some cajoling maybe some bribing to get the project completed. I was delighted to hear our local radio station coming through. Chris didn't care. He was off to another idea.

I think one of the advantages of homeschooling for him was the fact that he had large chunks of time for projects like the radio. Instead of a science project taking several weeks or a whole semester to complete in a regular school, he could do a fairly complicated project in a matter of a few hours or a few days. With little to distract him, he could stay focused if the interest level was high.

I mentioned before that each family member has had to become proficient in patience. Chris's older brother certainly had his share of "moments." In teaching situations, especially sports related, AJ was very good. He would patiently help Chris learn to kick a soccer ball in a specific direction. He would help Chris throw and catch a football. AJ was very supportive and would encourage Chris to improve and do his best during a game. I think AJ was Chris's number one fan. Since Chris was very tall for his age, he tended to be a bit uncoordinated. His eye-hand coordination wasn't the best either. So AJ was very helpful and creative in the sports arena. He would make up little games to teach Chris skills.

It wasn't always a one-sided situation. In spite of his tall frame, Chris developed very good balance and got pretty good at skateboarding. He eventually got the opportunity to teach AJ some skills in that sport. Now, that was a nice switch.

AJ was particularly patient when he had friends over and Chris wanted to be included. The friends seemed to like Chris and they included him in sleep-overs and "guy" activities. I suppose, to a certain degree, all those guys learned to be patient with Chris.

Phil had to be very patient, too. Often, Chris would want to do a "little" father-son project. Usually, the project Chris had in mind would take several hours, or days, requiring some special supplies. But Chris's cry was always, "Let's do it NOW, Dad." Phil would do his best with the impatient, stubborn request. Some projects worked out okay, some were much more crude than Phil would have liked, and some got put on the back burner until . . . well, until never. Chris would forget about them, or just didn't want to go to the store to purchase supplies. Phil always did his best to work with Chris and encourage him.

Phil has a way with words and he usually knew what words to use to bring out the best in Chris. That skill has been very effective. "You're doing a good job, Chris." "What if we try doing it this way?" "Are you sure that's the way this works best?" "What else can we do to make this better?" Phil's gentle encouraging words usually gave Chris reason to stop and think things through as he marched to his own drum.

Were we always patient? Heavens, no! There were many times when Phil and I had plans for a quiet evening, but Chris had a "project" in mind. There were times when AJ needed to study or was running out to class and Chris wanted his attention. There were times when I wanted to read and Chris wanted to talk. Sure, sometimes we told Chris to go do something else. Those things happen in all families. It just seems to happen more often with an energetic ADD/HD kid around. I often wished I could bottle up his energy so I could use a little.

Lesson #3 – Creativity

"They can because they think they can."

Virgil

I don't think of myself as particularly creative; however, having an ADHD kid around has necessitated that I use my creative side more regularly. Since I tend to be a "habit" type, I can allow myself to get into a rut, which is comfortable for me. Chris, however, needs to change it up. So what worked yesterday with him, didn't always work today.

This was especially true when homeschooling. Chris needed to have short, interesting and varied lessons using hands on activities. Now that really challenged me to be creative. I searched good school supply stores and book stores for activities that would give Chris a good learning opportunity and some fun. Often, we would work together to invent our own.

We always had board games on hand for family fun after dinner. Sometimes, it was just me and Chris playing, but it kept him from driving everyone crazy.

We would take walks around the neighborhood and look for something new or different. For a time, we lived in a pretty rural area. That gave us opportunities to see nature in a new light. Many times, Chris would ride his bike while I walked. And when new homes were being built in our area, we took walks to see what was taking place at different stages of the construction project. At times when we were driving to run an errand, if I saw something different or interesting, I would stop the car and we would take a good look. It made for good conversations and a teaching opportunity.

We had a forest fire not too far from our home one year. We used that as a topic for a speech, using pictures of the fire for the visual aid. Being active in Boy Scouts for a time gave us several opportunities to work on creative projects. Scouting helped Chris experience camping and other activities we may not have been involved with otherwise. He made a campfire for us in the middle of the sandbox one summer. He knew exactly how to do it, and we enjoyed an evening or two around the campfire, chatting and enjoying our time together.

Although Chris wasn't always keen on museums or long lines, I made it a point to get him out of the house to visit a local historical site or an apple orchard at apple-picking time. We even had an opportunity to watch filming of a major motion picture when the location was in our general area. He usually wasn't a "happy camper" on some of those excursion, but it helped give him some varied experiences and change the pace every now and then.

Now, Chris is a very creative guy. He liked building things; so blocks, pieces of wood or Legos became the most intricate creations. He built forts and battlefields for his little green army men. And he and AJ loved to make forts using tables, chairs, sofa cushions, and blankets. They became quite detailed, and on occasion, I was invited to crawl through them. A secret passage here and a maze there made for hours (days) of fun. Although our home was in disarray often with these creations, I have always felt a house is to be lived in, so I let the creative juices flow. I knew we would eventually get order back.

There was a time when he was getting into music that Chris would put on concerts for us. He would turn his room into a "stage" and invite us in. Of course, we had to pay to enter, but a quarter here and there made the evening more fun for him. Chris would play his favorite song, and dance his heart out. Often, the dancing turned into jumping off his bed. At one point, he made his dad get the old black light out and then he really put on a show!

In providing toys and free-time activities, I tried to find something that would be active and hopefully offer some educational purpose. He liked strategy type games, so we had several of those. He always beat me or his dad, but boy, could he and his older brother go at it! AJ was merciless; but Chris eventually got good enough to beat him fair and square.

As a teen, Chris found a website that allowed him to create music using various musical instrument sounds. He became quite adept at combining musical sounds into a melody. He would tweak his music to get just the right sound. I found his creations to be interesting and some were actually pretty good.

I truly believe ADD/HD kids are very intelligent. When they are given opportunities to use their intelligence in ways that are more in line with their natural bent, they really shine. ADD/HD kids just process things differently. Sadly, because it isn't the way most of the population do things, they tend to be seen as having a disability; however I have learned that when I give Chris leeway to do things his way, his intelligence and creativity come out in ways that often amaze me.

You have probably heard of all the famous people in history who were identified as ADD/HD or are suspected of having been

ADD/HD because of their behavior and difficulties in school. Their intelligence, creative nature, and persistence brought us many of the things we take for granted today. Einstein, Thomas Edison, Michael Phelps, Wolfgang Mozart, Henry Ford, and Elvis Presley are just a few. Our children are like many of these famous people. They tend to be full of ideas, and they want to accomplish them right now. They don't see obstacles the way we do. And they have energy to spare. If we can help our child channel his/her ideas and energy, we can train them to use that natural creativity and intelligence in good ways. When they find an activity that really speaks to them like music, art, writing, or sports, we want to give them every opportunity to excel in that area. We need to be careful not to discourage them or stifle that creativity. Who knows . . . our child may be the next inventor of something that changes our world in a way that makes it much better or who inspires others to reach their dreams.

Lesson #4 – Outside Activities

"The wisdom of life consists in the elimination of nonessentials."

Lin Yutang

Speaking of outside activities like sports, theatre, and the others, it's important to be sure our child is truly interested. As you already know, an ADD/HD kid has a short attention span. So committing to an activity that may not work for our child can be costly and quite frustrating. Since our older son was very athletic, it was natural for us to get Chris involved in sports, too. However, Chris was very awkward as a young boy. His body just didn't respond instantly to the prompting of his brain to jump or pivot or kick. Consequently, he was often just a split second behind the play on the field or court. He appeared not to be paying attention, but, in fact, his reaction time was slow. Since he wasn't a coach's dream player at that point in his life, he would get only the required playing time. He saw himself as a star athlete; the coach did not. So, he often sat on the bench. Eventually, he would want to quit, but we always insisted he finish out the season, usually with much complaining and frustration. We wanted him to know that once he committed, he had to see it through. After a couple of team experiences, he opted out. No more soccer or basketball for him.

We went on to music. He wanted to play drums, but Dad nixed that idea. We settled on guitar and soon, we were spending time and money at the local music store where lessons were offered. Again, Chris couldn't or wouldn't focus when practice time came around. He wanted to play his favorite song by his third lesson. Uh, I don't think so.

Chris and his guitar teacher became good buddies and Chris enjoyed being there. Sadly, though, not much learning took place mostly because Chris wouldn't practice between lessons. He couldn't stay focused when practice became monotonous.

In middle school, Chris became interested in skateboarding. It was a great activity to keep him physically busy and outdoors getting lots of sunshine and fresh air. Considering his lanky frame, Chris actually got quite good. At the time, there was an indoor-outdoor skateboard park nearby and he spent time regularly riding the ramps and learning how to do jumps. Since he was one of the few young guys who could skate during the day, he was befriended by the employees who showed him some great tricks. He loved it. It was one of the few activities he stayed with long term, probably because there were so many different maneuvers to learn. Over and over he would try a jump or special trick. After a few skinned elbows and knees, he could skate with the best of them.

I think it is important to help our child find something that he or she really excels at and help them stick to it. It can be a source of excitement and self-acceptance. When we excel at something, we feel good about ourselves. That will go a long way in helping our child develop a peer group that accepts and befriends him or her. If our child feels like he or she doesn't belong, it can affect their self-image and the way they relate to others. As they find a place and group where they fit in like everyone else, they can see their goodness. That will help them move into other arenas knowing they have the capacity to succeed.

I have a dear friend whose grandson has had some difficult times in school. In searching for an outside activity for him, they discovered theatre. It's amazing how he will go to rehearsals over and over and act appropriately for two or three hours at a time because he loves to perform. It has given him an outlet for his creative side; he is having fun and being successful in something that is important in our community; and it helps use up energy that might otherwise be a problem. He truly shines in that area of his young life. It has also given him a group of friends outside of school.

On the other side of the coin, we need to be careful not to overdo the outside activities. I truly believe children need down-time. I know down-time can be stressful with an ADD/HD kid in the house. It seems that is when unhappy incidences occur. However, too much going on can be crazy making when we are driving all over town and are rarely home. Controlling that can keep our child from getting over stimulated, and it will save our sanity.

Lesson #5 – Screen Time

"You must have discipline to have fun"

Julia Child

My biggest admonition with an ADD/HD child is to limit "screen" time. In this day and age of TV being a baby sitter or distraction while we cook dinner or do other necessary tasks, it's easy to just turn it on and have our child sit for several minutes. Or more to the point, does our child have a WII, Play Station, Nintendo, other computer game system, or, heaven forbid, their own smart phone? These are all technologies that we have been brainwashed to think we HAVE TO have. I know they are fun, and they keep a child interested and occupied. However, I believe they are a technology that can work against us, especially with ADD/HD children. The images on the screen change quickly and the games offer immediate rewards. They keep the brain very stimulated. I believe it is easy for ADD/HD children to get addicted to these games. These addictions make it harder for our child to concentrate when the pace is slower and the rewards take time to materialize, like in the classroom. There is limited research on this topic, but everything I've read suggests that ADD/HD children are especially prone to addiction to internet games. Wow, our child already has a problem focusing and staying on track, who wants to make that more difficult for him or her?

In some situations, it isn't necessary to take those games away. Many of these games can be educational. We had several math and strategy games that Chris played through the computer and internet. He also improved his reading skills when he had to go over game instructions and rules to play the game well. However, it would help to limit the time spent on them. I suggest setting an amount of time that is reasonable. Then give the child a choice of when he or she wants the screen time. Perhaps they want an hour now as opposed to 30 minutes now and 30 minutes after dinner. Or they have to finish chores before screen time. The limit needs to be firm.

Technology should not be in their room. The temptation will be very hard to resist for any child. A parent needs to resist all negotiations for more time on the game, unless to use that as an incentive. We need to keep in mind that we are the parent and we have final say. I know, I know. This can be really hard. However, as persistent as our child may be, our "no" should mean "NO." Actually, that goes for any situation. If we waver at all, we are toast. That child will sense our weakness and go in for the kill. We cannot let that happen. We need to be firm.

I speak from experience. We did not place many limits on Chris's screen time; mostly because as a homeschooled kid, he had more free time than regular school kids. We also allowed him to have his games and computer in his room. I can't tell you how often I found him playing a game in the middle of the night. I tell you, that is not a good thing! Once the addiction took hold, it was impossible to break. He became anti-social to a certain extent; all he wanted to do was play a computer game. That made homeschooling him harder. It limited the time he wanted to spend with friends. Often, Chris would run out of his room at mealtime, stuff himself as quickly as possible, then run back to his game.

I'm embarrassed to tell you this story. It was a time when both my husband and I were weak, and didn't want to fight it. The addiction caught hold of Chris before our very eyes when we didn't see it happen. Or, maybe we didn't want to see it happen.

I have since learned that video game developers design the games to be addicting. After all, these are money-making ventures. They start with simple graphics and basic activities, then the games get faster, with better graphics, and, often, more violence. From their point of view, the name of the game is profits.

As busy parents, we sometimes look the other way, don't we? Well, I'm here to strongly encourage parents to be courageous and stick to whatever rules are set. Before long, our child will know when we mean business and when we can be "squeezed" for more. We need to know where we want to draw the line, then stand firm. Yes, that ADD/HD child of ours can and will wear us down. However, it will make the long term better, and our child will respect us for that. Now, that doesn't mean it will be easy; but eventually, a mutual understanding will transpire and life will get better. The difficult times will have been well worth the hassle, and we will look back and be grateful for the strength and wisdom to persevere. I have known families who have to make their homes video game-free zones to prevent or stop addictive behavior. We have to be willing to do what it takes. Plus, video/computer games can be real time wasters. They take valuable time away from other activities that may serve our child better.

How did we get the addiction lessened? Actually, Chris decided on his own in his late teens that he needed to be a more serious student. He began limiting his screen time, and spent more time on school-work. Having a girlfriend helped. As he spent time with her, he didn't miss the games as much. When we talk about it now, he says it was hard to begin disciplining himself since he was allowed to play whenever he wanted. Now, he sees himself as growing more mature, and that means doing what needs to be done when it needs to be done. He will play a game with friends every now and then, but the addictive behavior is gone, thank goodness.

7

Moving Forward

"The best thing about the future is that it comes only one day at a time."

Abraham Lincoln

What can I say to you as you go through that "daily grind" to help you? As you already know, having children and raising them well is a huge labor of love. I think when we first decide to have a baby, we think of those sweet smelling, smiling babies in commercials. The commercials don't show the unhappy baby who just cries and cries and nothing we do helps. The commercials don't show us as haggardly walking the baby in the middle of the night. They don't convey the "fragrance" of a poopy diaper or spit-up. Perhaps, a family member has had a baby recently, and our hearts yearn for one, too. However, when that little cherub arrives, we are shocked that the fantasy doesn't last very long – a day or two maybe . . . or little spurts here and there. We laugh because it's the truth.

Yes, you already know how difficult it is to be a parent. Not that there aren't just as many joys, if not more. Having an ADD/HD child just adds to the labor of love. I believe the most important thing we can do is see our child as a gift. Not necessarily the gift we asked for or wanted, but a gift nonetheless. When we can look at our child with eyes that see goodness, innocence, and lovability, half the battle is won.

I dislike using the word "battle", but sometimes it feels that way, don't you agree? We certainly don't want to see our child as the enemy. This isn't a battle between me and my child. Sometimes, it's a battle between me and myself. . .when I'm tired and stretched to the max and I can't stir up the energy to help with homework or referee one more argument between siblings. Sometimes it's a battle between me and the clock. There never seems to be enough time to do everything I need to do for my family, my child, and myself. Our child is not battling us. He or she doesn't mean to be flighty or fidgety. Our child doesn't bounce from this to that on purpose. That's just the way it is. The sooner we accept our child "as is," the sooner we can stop fighting the situation and just work with it for our child's benefit as well as our own. We have a saying in our house when things don't go quite right. We say, "That's just the way it is." And, yes, with our ADD/HD child, "that's just the way it is."

There will be extended family and friends who get frustrated with our child. They don't understand and they feel bad for us. I remember my mother telling me things like "Poor you. You have to deal with Chris," or "Why can't you make him sit still?" I eventually just told

Mom that we had it under control. She looked at me with skepticism, but never made a comment again. Those situations made me feel bad, but I knew we were doing the best we could.

We often felt odd in public because of Chris's behavior. Try as we did, sometimes his behavior just wasn't fitting in as we would have liked. We got to the point of not making excuses. We just figured people would accept him and us or not. Oh, well. Really, this touches the heart of our ego. Yes, our self-image can have such a huge effect on us – what we do, where we live, how we dress, what we have. It all comes down to how we see ourselves, and how we want others to see us. It's a big deal. So, if our child isn't just perfect, or close to it in behavior and appearance, it affects how we feel about ourselves. However, when we accept our child unconditionally, we give "ego" the boot to a certain extent. We allow our child to be freely who he is and not place pressure to perform or behave in a manner that is virtually impossible for him. It's very freeing for our child and for us.

When I got to that place, I found myself more relaxed. I enjoyed Chris more. I could laugh at his antics not at him, but with him because he really was a joyful little boy. I found him fun to be with. The more I relaxed and let go of ego, the more I enjoyed him.

One thing we tried to do for Chris is not to label him. For a long time, we didn't emphasize the "ADHD". We believed it was important for him to see himself as a "normal" kid. Actually, I do believe he is normal with a few challenges different from what others may face. I mean, really, don't we all have a challenge or two of some sort? There are so many ways in which we all are different that I sometimes wonder if labels serve any purpose, at least in some areas of life. Not long ago, I asked Chris a few questions about what he remembers as an ADHD young boy. I thought his response to one question in particular was quite telling. He said, "Lucky for you, Mom, that I have grown out of my ADHD or whatever you want to call it." I think it's healthy for him not to see himself with that label. That way, he has no excuses for not working hard, rising to the challenges of life, or pushing himself to be a better person. Although I sometimes worry about ADD/HD making some of his choices harder, I am so proud of him for moving on with life like anyone else would be expected to do. Actually, I believe he has outgrown the hyperactivity. He isn't a "squirrely" adult, but he can be very high energy when he wants to be. I believe he has learned to channel his energy to serve him better. When that happens, it's his choice. Big difference!

As an adult, Chris still has unrealistic expectations. We see this when he sets a high goal and really believes he can achieve it in record time. Example: Every few months, Chris will decide he needs to buff out a little. He wants more muscle on his arms and legs. Well, as a very tall man (six foot seven inches), with long arms and legs, he probably won't ever look like one of those buffed out athletes. But he wants to try. Our only admonition at this point is "Don't hurt yourself." So away he goes to his weight bench and begins an ardent weight training program. After about three or four days, he's ready to measure his biceps to see how well he has improved the size of his muscles. If it isn't a noticeable difference in a few days, he gets disappointed. Sometimes he will give up because the reason for his new-found fitness gig isn't important enough. However, if it's really important to him, he may stick with it for a couple of weeks, maybe a month. As you can see, that expectation is unrealistic and he is hard pressed to stick to the regimen if the goal isn't met in his time frame. Time and again, his dad has counseled him to stick with it, no matter what the goal or the difficulty. More often than not, his attention is diverted to the next project.

Chris has changed his mind about a career choice a few times, too. At one point, he got interested in fire science and wanted to be an emergency medical tech. He enrolled in a course that had an excellent reputation for high student success. Unfortunately, after only two or three weeks and a substantial amount of financial investment, he left the class for various reasons. Then he wanted to enroll in a local radiology tech course. That was a major program of study and an even greater investment. We insisted he do as much research as possible before enrolling. We are happy he found some information about the program that caused us to rethink the plan. There have been a few more of those instances. That "focus" thing is a tough one.

In his late teens, Chris met a nice young lady who became his girlfriend. I worried that she wouldn't accept him once she got to know and experience his ADHD tendencies. However, she has completely accepted him. She helps him with school-work and she just loves his funny side. Chris is a very caring young man. He cares for her in ways that meet her needs from a relationship. Together, they are delightful for us to watch. As I write this, they are engaged and planning to wed after both graduate university.

Chris attended a local community college for a quarter or two. Although he enjoyed the camaraderie of one or two classmates, became friends with the teacher, and did well, he was very frustrated with the challenge of driving to the campus, searching for a parking space, and getting to class on time. It was also very disappointing when he could not get into the classes he needed in order to move on because of the large enrollment in the community college system. His desire to get a degree led him to research online universities. He found one that appears to be meeting his needs. He is able to do the coursework at his own pace within set deadlines, and the quarter system makes it possible to complete the courses before he loses interest. He is required to interact with classmates through online forums. Posts and comments on the forum have certain requirements and boundaries, so he is challenged to be thoughtful and use what is learned in class regularly. He has a great deal of reading and research for each class. I'm sure it takes him longer to complete assignments than it does for most students. However, he is experiencing a great deal of success and he is enjoying the challenge. He especially likes the fact that he doesn't have to fight for a parking space.

What is wonderful is he feels good about himself and relishes each success. He is hopeful for the future and sees himself succeeding. Isn't that what we all desire as parents? Yes, we want a future full of hope for every one of our children. My husband and I weren't sure he would stay the course and succeed at the college level. We were concerned he would lose interest and look for something else to do. However, he has an A- grade average so far and shows no signs of giving up. He is interested in psychology/psychiatry. Probably so he can help ADD/HD kids in the future. Now, how good is THAT?

8

If I Could Do It Over

"Hindsight is always 20/20"

Billy Wilder

In reflecting back over the years of raising Chris, there are some things I would do differently, or more of, if I could do it all over again.

I would worry less about a clean house and more about meaningful conversations.

I would hug our sons more, and tell them more often how much I love them and how proud I am of them.

I would write more little notes of encouragement for our sons.

I would encourage our ADHD son to spend more time with friends and arrange more get-togethers.

I would turn the TV off and encourage family fun time instead.

I would plan more outings for our family to do together.

I would limit screen time in a major way and keep the computer out of our son's room so we could monitor that activity better.

I would require daily reading for enjoyment as part of our day.

I would "lighten up," not be so serious, laugh a lot more, and really enjoy myself and our sons.

The good thing about hindsight is you can use those insights to improve the future. So, as I read over that list, I see some things I can continue to do now. That will give me a happy heart and I know it will warm our sons' hearts as well.

Years ago, as a college student, I read a poem by Kahlil Gibran titled "On Children." It was written almost a century ago and is included in Gibran's book, The Prophet. I thought the poem was interesting when I first read it. I recently came across the poem again. Now, as I read it from a parent's point of view, I find its words so much more meaningful. It is a reminder that our job as parents is to prepare our children then send them forth to live their lives just as we have lived ours. Below is an excerpt from the poem I find particularly touching.

"You are the bows from which your children
as living arrows are sent forth.
The archer sees the mark upon the path of the infinite,
and He bends you with His might
that His arrows may go swift and far.
Let your bending in the archer's hand be for gladness;
For even as He loves the arrow that flies,
so He loves also the bow that is stable."

Looking through Chris's scrapbook, I was reminded of all the ups and downs we have been through, and it gave me the assurance that all is well. For, as hard a job as it has been, we have made it; and you will, too.

CPSIA information can be obtained at www.ICGtesting.com
Printed in the USA
LVOW060147150513

333657LV00005B/5/P

9 781625 170873